HOW TO LOCATE

AND USE

MANORIAL RECORDS

by

PATRICK PALGRAVE-MOORE B.A., F.S.A., F.S.G.

elvery
dowers

First published 1985
Elvery Dowers Publications
ISBN 0 9506290 2 2

printed in England by
W.H. Hutchins, Norwich, Norfolk.

Elvery Dowers Publications
13 West Parade, Norwich, Norfolk, NR2 3DN.
Telephone - Norwich (0603) 611336

Introduction

From parish registers and from census returns after 1841 it is a simple matter to compile a family tree of two, sometimes three generations which can be said to be proven beyond doubt. From the admission registers of borough freemanry it is possible to build up a proven family tree for as many generations as the freemanry was held, often to four or five generations. However, from the records of the manorial courts, it is possible to compile a family tree, proven beyond doubt, covering the span of centuries, provided the same land was held by the same family. Nowhere in the vast source material available to the researcher does this opportunity present itself better than in manorial records. Yet what do we find? Select any general textbook on genealogy published in the last fifty years and you will be lucky to find more than a casual mention of manorial records, at the most perhaps a page devoted to the subject. Is it no wonder then that this source, probably the most important of all sources has been so badly neglected? Undoubtedly, in the past, misconceptions have grown around the subject. Many still believe that their ancestors were 'ordinary folk' therefore manorial records could not possibly apply to their searches. Others believe that because they have only taken their tree back to the nineteenth century, manorial records for them have no relevance. Certainly it is true that the more land held by an ancestor, the more likely are their names to be found within the records but even quite humble families held at least some land and their names are as likely to be recorded as those of the great lords. The part played by luck is in their chance of survival through the centuries.

This book then attempts to sweep away the misconceptions surrounding the subject with its aura of scholarly limitation. In doing so, I have briefly described the make-up of the manorial system, its records, where they may be located and how they may be used in terms of genealogical research. I must clearly emphasise here that the book is not intended as a guide for academic historians but has been written primarily with the object of furthering interest in genealogical research.

In compiling this booklet I am grateful for the helpful comments received from Francis Minns and Stephen Bate.

The Manorial System

The history and development of any Society has tended to show an evolvement of its members into an organised economic unit for survival. From such units evolved leaders who might consolidate their positions into hereditary rights, subject nevertheless, to being supplanted by rival leaders. Anglo Saxon England had already established such units as villages with leaders effectively controlling the destiny of their inhabitants. The Norman invasion created a new warrior class of leaders for whom, the existing Saxon villages provided a natural unit for manorial grants in recognition of services rendered. Dispossession of over 90% of the Saxon gentry by a military aristocracy was extended by grants of new manors capable of being supported by a population of freemen, husbandmen or villeins, and serfs. This transposition also created a more lasting and systematic method of organising the unit. Manorial land was divided into two categories: the Lord's demesne, land for the support of his personal household and tenanted land granted to the villeins in return for services on the demesne. In the period following the Conquest, the treatment of serfs was not far removed from that of slaves and even the position of the villeins was one of subservience.

The manor operated an open field system of agriculture, divided into strips. The standard unit for each villein was a virgate, about thirty acres, though in East Anglia unique social conditions ascribed to the influx of Scandinavian ideas uses a standard measure of about twelve acres. Services due by the villeins were certainly less arduous than those imposed on the serfs, involving some ten days work each month, but their holdings, although gradually evolving into a semi-hereditary right, were still subject to the legal powers of the Lord, a power often exercised over life and death itself, with little redress. Free men, often with fixed rents, were free to leave the Lord's domain and choose another Lord as their service was more personal than agricultural. However, many freeholders, sometimes the Lords themselves, held manorial land of one or more manors in addition to their freeholds and technically would have been subject to the same obligations of service.

Continuity of the Lord's patronage enabled him to exact payment from his workers for certain everyday occurrences. For example, when a tenant's daughter was married, he exacted a tax known as a **merchate**. When a tenant died a **heriot** was levied and when the heirs came to take up the property another payment called a **relief** was charged. In the rare event that a Lord allowed a tenant to live outside the manorial boundaries the privilege was paid for with a **chevage**. As each parcel of land was conveyed from one tenant to another, the Lord in his role as owner, technically regranted the property to the new owner, subject to a payment known as a **fine**. This perhaps over-simplification of the order of society must be qualified to understand the extent of a manorial holding. Just as one manorial holding could extend into one or more villages, so could one village contain more than one manor, each lord having a claim on the services of the peasantry.

The system was hardly popular and not unnaturally, the peasantry eventually resisted. However at a time of increasing population and a great demand for land the Lord was able to meet such resistance with force, evicting those unwilling to yield to his terms. The Peasants Revolt of the fourteenth century did at least make the Lord aware that forced labour was not economically expedient and a system gradually evolved to commute services due for a payment of money, a consequence of which was a great increase in the Lords' income. The devastation of the countryside caused by the effects of the Black Death and the ensuing plagues completely changed the social fabric. As demand for land fell, so the demand for labour rose. The severity of this sudden devastation gave the labourers a strong hand and the Lords were forced to accept that they had to increase wage rates and give greater security to their tenants holdings.

From the fifteenth century, tenants were granted holdings with full hereditary rights and fixed rents. They received a copy of the entry recorded in the Lords manor records, their holding then being referred to as copy-hold. Profits from the Lords holdings did not keep pace with inflation. To counteract this he began selling parts of his demesne to neighbouring tenants and to a growing and aspiring band of merchants wishing to invest in property. Many a visitation family owes its gentle origins to one prosperous member of an otherwise humble family, whose fortune was made from the wealth created by the expanding trade of town and City.

To ensure a smooth running of the manorial unit, members of the Lord's community were elected or appointed to offices, each with a functional position to aid that community. The **steward** had charge of the records of the manor, for holding the Lord's courts and of complying with the legal complexities of land conveyancing. By the eighteenth century this office tended to become the role of the provincial lawyer who often performed the office and passed on the role to a successor.
The **Bailiff** was the Lord's agent and general overseer of his estate. The **Reeve** was responsible for the cultivation of the lands, the sale of stock and grain and was usually appointed from one of the Lord's copyholders. The **Hayward** had specific responsibilities for the Lord's woods, corn and meadows. The **Constable**, an unpopular office,was elected usually annually to keep the peace, to summon men to jury service and to supervise the pound, the latter sometimes under the control of a **Pindar**. When the office of constable in relation to the Lord's dwindling number of tenants seemed anachronistic, the office became subject to appointment by the parish vestry. Perhaps one of the few offices that might be sought after was that of the **Ale Taster**. He had to ensure that a good standard of beer was produced, a practice which in later centuries became subservient to the main task of ensuring that those wishing to make the ale, paid their licence fees to the Lord.

Throughout the subsequent centuries the manorial system survived as a focal point for village life with the Lord or squire as its central figurehead. As Lord, he continued to exercise his manorial authority over his tenants though by the end of the eighteenth century this had been reduced to nothing more than a token gesture. The enclosing of open fields and common lands which permeated Georgian England further reduced the need for any judicial overseer, as more and more of the smaller tenants were bought out by larger landowners. Invariably, the Lord was appointed a local magistrate and indirectly widened his sphere of judicial authority, but the everyday affairs of the village became more centered around meetings of the parish vestry. Enfranchisement of the remaining copyhold land into freeholds on payment of a fee and a series of Statutes during the nineteenth century led in 1926 to the final abolition of the copyhold form of tenure.

Today, the Lordship remains a conveyable property in name only, stripped of its ancient rights and privileges, although in a few cases, some have retained their rights over common lands, mineral extraction and a handful still retain honours linked to services to the Crown.

Manorial Documents

Records associated with the manor are numerous. Some of these fell into disuse many centuries ago and it is unlikely that many family historians will have cause to refer to these. This book then deals with the principal sources of use in family research. Let us first consider in what the Lord was primarily interested. He needed to know who owed him money and services, when they became due, and when they were paid. He also had to exercise jurisdiction over the tenants and inhabitants of the manorial land, a special jurisdiction devolved from the Crown. These two functions, most often held one after the other at the same Court hearing were known as a Court Leet and a Court Baron. The Court Leet heard criminal offences not punishable by Common Law usually then referred to the Assizes, and offences involving sums of money of over 40/- in worth. There is a general mis-belief that all offences were heard at the Court Leet and property transactions at the Court Baron. The Court Baron, the tenants own Court to ensure the smooth running of the community was also empowered to deal with minor and common law offences and for issues involving 40/-

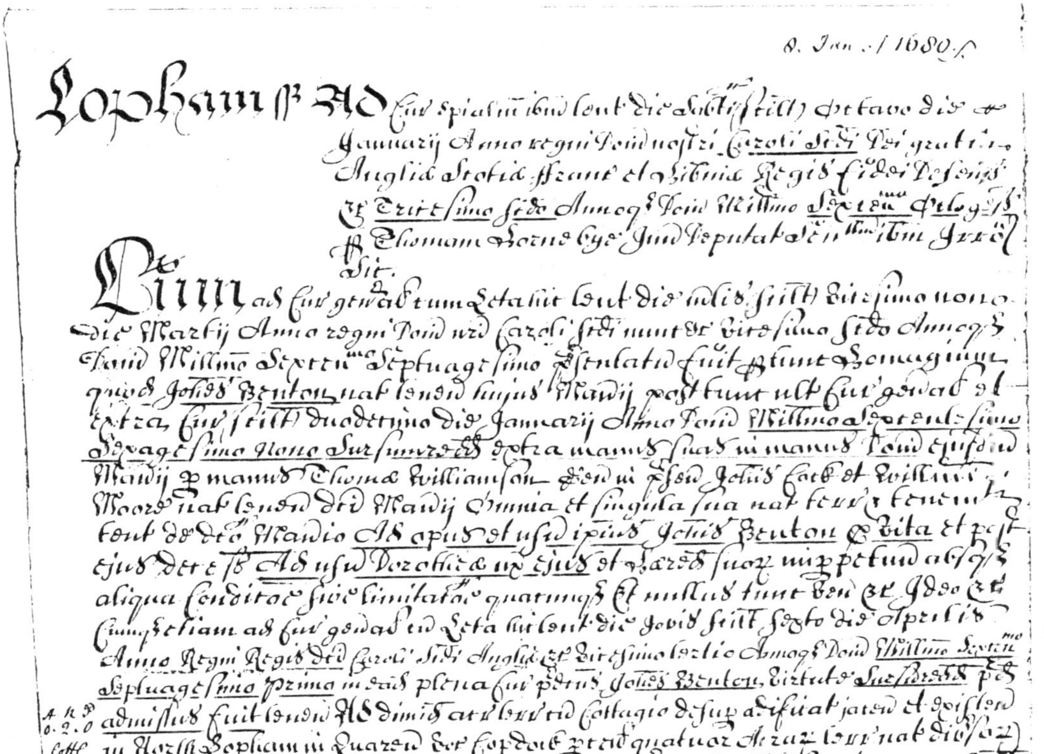
8. Jan. 1680/1

Lopham ss Ad Cur' spial[e]m ibid[em] tent' die Sabbati scilt octavo die Januarij Anno regni Dni nostri Caroli Sc'di Dei gratia Angliae Scotiae Franc' et Hibernie Regis fidei Defensoris &c Tricesimo Sc'do Annoq[ue] Dni Millmo Sexcen[tesi]mo Octog[esi]mo

Ad Cur' general' tum Leta ibid[em] tent' die Lune scilt vicesimo nono die Martij Anno regni Dni nri Caroli Sc'di nunc &c vicesimo Sc'do Annoq[ue] Dni Millmo Sexcen[tesi]mo Septuagesimo presentatu fuit p[er] tunc homagium quod Johes Benton nat' tenens huius Manerij ...

Fig. 1. Manor of Lopham, Norfolk 8.1.1680/1.
Copy admission of Dorothy Benton on the death of her husband John to property John had on the death of his sister Rose Benton 1639. (ex Libris Norfolk & Norwich Genealogical Society)

The Manor of Thornham. { Rental of the Quit Rents which became due to the Lord of the said Manor on old Michaelmas Day 1847

Tenants' Names &c.	Amt. Rent £	s	d	Years rent due	Head Silver Money £	s	d	Total £	s	d	Received £	s	d	Remarks
Allen John Thornham		.	1	5	.	.	4	.	.	9				
~~Allen Willm & Wife, late Steeles, d^o~~														
~~Allen Willm, d^o, late Stantons~~														
Benton Joseph, Manchester, late Henry Benton's	.	16	10½											
D^o, late Butlers	.	2	6											
	.	19	4½	5	.	.	4	4	17	2½				
Bunn Mary Thornham, late John Bunn's	.	1	5½	5	.	.	4	.	7	7½		7	7½	
Bunting Frances, d^o, late Thomas Bunting's	.	1	5	5	.	.	4	.	7	5		7	5	
Bunting Ann d^o late d^o	.	.	5	5	.	.	4	.	2	5		2	5	
Bowler Willm d^o for part late Spanton's														
Breeden George Holkham, late Spanton's Executors		7	8	5			4	1	18	8				[illegible] Sept [illegible]

Fig. 2. Manor of Thornham, Norfolk. Rental 1847
(ex Libris Norfolk & Norwich Genealogical Society)

or less. The main business of the Court Baron however was to note changes in property ownership and it is this category which proves so valuable to the family historian. This was the category in which the Lord had more of a vested interest as he was able to claim payments for each transaction.

Early court records were written on both sides of long sheets of parchment, sewn together then rolled together for ease of storage. Records of later centuries came to be written firstly in MINUTE BOOKS, many of which serve as prime source material in the absence of the originals, then copied into parchment leaved bound books. Often, these court rolls and court books overlap one another and occasionally one might find a duplicate set of records written contemporarily with the originals. It was from this class of record that the term COPYHOLD evolved. When tenants were admitted to their property they were given a copy of the entry appearing in the court records. Thus they held BY COPY. These copy admissions (Fig. I) form another category of manorial records but because they were given to the tenant they are more likely found with other title deeds lodged with local solicitors or now with estate collections.

One must not forget that although court rolls and books form the most important record of the manor, other official records can often be of great use to the historian. COURT VERDICTS, or decisions of the court often appear as separate documents. RENTALS (Fig. 2) often filed in consecutive years, sometimes found within the court book pages, are a useful record to trace particular individuals over a period of land ownership. Surveys of property often containing drawings and maps enable a more accurate identification of particular property. Docquet Books or Indexes are sometimes found as separate documents, usually limited to the names of those being admitted to property, but more likely, these, if they exist, will be found either at the commencement or at the end of each court book.

How to Locate the Records

It will prove useful at first to discover what exactly you are looking for. Remember that several manors may be involved in a particular area and a preliminary study of published local history works should give a listing of these. Remember also that the chances of survival for records over several

centuries must be small, so do not expect immediate success. Many will have been destroyed, particularly those of the mediaeval period, some will have been split up, some will be simply lost.
In a number of families, court records have been lovingly preserved and passed down from generation to generation. The current trend however seems to result in records being sold to owners far removed from their place of origin.
Once it is known which manors are sought, contact should be made with your local Record Office. Most of these offices have now begun a list of manorial records in their possession and often extend this to list those known in other locations.

If unsuccessful, contact the present Lord of the Manor, who may well have possession of the records in his home. I shall say something of this later but at this stage contact cannot be made unless the identity of the present Lord is readily known. It should be noted that not all manors are held by individuals. Many were in the hands of institutions such as Oxbridge Colleges and Ecclesiastical authorities. For example see Fig. 3.

The next enquiry should be directed to the MANORIAL DOCUMENTS REGISTER. This is a list of manors arranged by County with details of the category and location of each data source. This is an official list and comes within the jurisdiction of the Master of the Rolls. The Index is housed at Quality House, Quality Court, Chancery Lane, London. Only personal visits are suggested but specific written queries will be answered. There is an obvious overlap with the listings provided by local record offices but information is being updated regularly. Sadly however, the sales of Lordships and their records have meant a dislocation of the information filed and although every effort is made to obtain details of new purchases the sometimes secretive nature of these transactions makes this difficult. There are in fact rules governing the possession of these documents. The Lord has to ensure safe keeping, advise their location and any change of ownership and ensure the records do not leave or return, rules unfortunately not always observed.

Assuming by this stage that particular records have not been located there are still a few avenues worth following. The latest publication of Kelly's directories for each County, usually 1937, will give the name of the then Lord of each manor. It may be possible to identify that individual with a family of the name at the same address. A polite enquiry will soon determine if records are still held, their location and content, or whether the identify of the new owner is known.
Invariably, the family will have moved away, taking with them their manorial records to be lodged with family solicitors in some distant part of the country. If an old landed family, an entry in Burke's Landed Gentry or Burke's Peerage may show the address of the present head of the family.

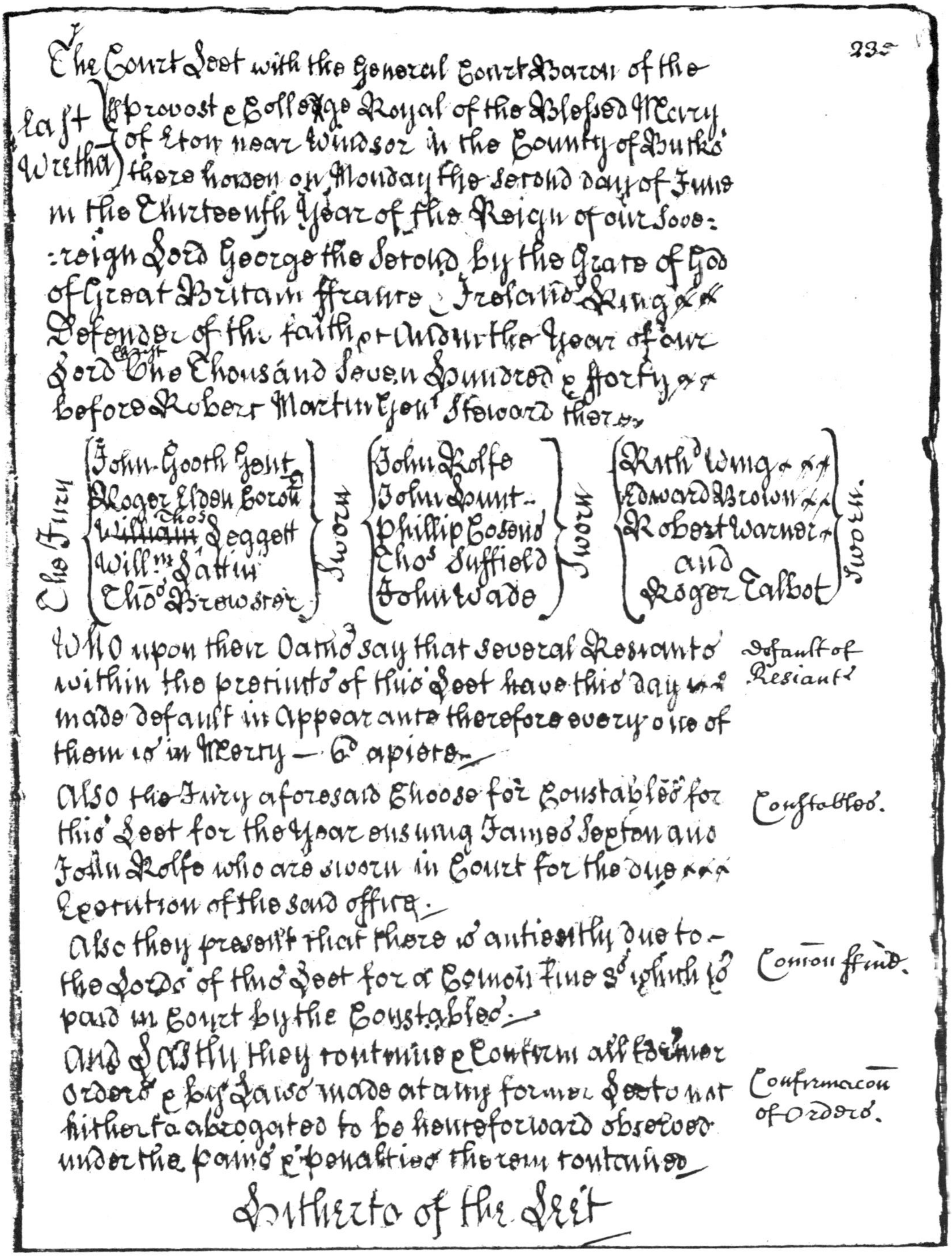

232

East Wretham — The Court Leet with the General Court Baron of the Provost & College Royal of the Blessed Mary of Eton near Windsor in the County of Bucks there holden on Monday the second day of June in the Thirteenth Year of the Reign of our Sove-reign Lord George the Second by the Grace of God of Great Britain ffrance & Ireland King &c Defender of the faith &c And in the Year of our Lord One Thousand Seven Hundred & fforty &c before Robert Martin Gent Steward there

The Jury: John Gooch Gent, Roger Eldon Gent, ~~William~~ Thos Leggett, Willm Sattin, Thos Brewster — Sworn; John Rolfe, John Hunt, Phillip Cosens, Thos Suffield, John Wade — Sworn; Richd Wing, Edward Brown, Robert Warner and Roger Talbot — Sworn

Who upon their Oaths say that several Resiants within the precincts of this Leet have this day made default in Appearance therefore every one of them is in Mercy — 6d apiece — Default of Resiants

Also the Jury aforesaid Choose for Constables for this Leet for the Year ensuing James Sexton and John Rolfe who are sworn in Court for the due Execution of the said office. — Constables.

Also they present that there is anciently due to the Lords of this Leet for a Comon fine 8d which is paid in Court by the Constables — Comon ffine.

And Lastly they continue & Confirm all former Orders & by Laws made at any former Leets not hitherto abrogated to be henceforward observed under the pains & penalties therein contained — Confirmacon of Orders.

Hitherto of the Leet

Fig. 3. Manor of East Wretham, Norfolk. 2nd June 1740
Entry from the court book showing the format used in the preamble. Note that the Lord of the Manor in this case is the Provost and College Royal at Eton, Bucks.

A further enquiry may be made at the offices of the Manorial Society. Founded in 1906 and publishing a journal for its members, the Society is often aware of the identity of new purchasers of Lordships though it should be remembered it is under no obligation to disclose their identity. Application should be made to The Manorial Society of Great Britain, 65 Belmont Hill, London SE13 5AX.

As a last resort, there is the unenviable task of locating local solicitors in the vicinity of the manor in the hope that the records may have been lodged with them. Quite often the older law firms are successors of earlier Stewards to the Manors and their records become deposited with them for safe keeping. Quite often nowadays, solicitors have little time to spend on enquiries of this nature, invariably have no knowledge of what records are held and even if known, need approval of clients before disclosing information therefrom. Even there the matter is not so simple. In some cases, records have been held for so long that the identity of the client has been lost. Quite often this will deter solicitors even from depositing the material in record offices. The problem here is serious but is one that can result in searchers 'going around in circles' trying to get correct information. For the moment, there is no answer. One cannot force solicitors to surrender documents if unwilling, neither can they be enforced to maintain such records in suitable storage. There will be occasions in which the researcher will have to accept that either the record does not exist or if it does, he or she is not going to be allowed access.

For those researchers who have reached far back into their ancestral past, there is some glimmer of hope. Whilst it is true that the older the record the less the chance of survival, there is a large collection of court rolls housed in the Public Record Office. These have been listed by HM Stationery Office (1896) and copies may be found in the more important reference libraries.

What you may expect to find

The first thing that becomes apparent in the court rolls and early court books is that they are written in latin. This in itself might deter many enthusiasts and no doubt is the principal reason why this source has been so little used in the past. Whilst a knowledge of latin is obviously an advantage, it need not deter the enthusiast willing to make an effort to understand the system. During the period of the Commonwealth and after 1733 these records were written in English and it is a useful first step to spend some time examining these periods in the records to become acclimatised to the fairly standard phraseology used. The style and format of the English is identical to that of the latin, and very quickly you will be able to determine just where the important parts of the text lie and which parts of legal jargon can be ignored.

The heading for each court (Fig. 3) gives the name of the manor, the type of court, the name of the Lord and the date. For those searching families who actually held the manor, this can sometimes be misleading, especially where descent of the manor has passed through several generations bearing the same Christian name. Many an early pedigree has been concocted on this basis drawing completely wrong conclusions. A roll of those who should be present was then called and those absent were fined a nominal sum depending on the validity of their excuse if any. The words ESSOINS or DEFAULT OF TENANTS usually appears here as a marginal entry. Then comes the list of jurymen known as the Homage, usually drawn from local farmers, duly sworn in to act as adjudicators over the court business. A list of complaints follows, criminal offences for the court leet and common law offences for the court baron, the latter recording such punishments as the pillory, the stocks or fines. These offences which to us would seem quite trivial can be most informative to the family historian. It is from these that an ancestor's character may be discovered. Finally, comes the important business of the court, to record changes in ownership of land. For the genealogist, it is this part that will become most rewarding. To take an extreme example, if a family held a particular piece of land, no matter how small, over several centuries, and the manorial records covering that property can be found, then it is possible to find enough information within the records to draw up a family tree, provable beyond any doubt. How many data sources can it be said are so obliging?

When a tenant died, his death was reported to the next court sitting. Up to three proclamations were then usually made at three successive sittings, each asking for the heir to the deceased to attend the court and be admitted to the property. If none came, the property reverted to the lord, although the lord would often regrant at a later date if the heir came forward. Where property was widely held, it could not always have been easy to ensure that an heir was notified of his entitlement. However the system prevailed. The heir might attend the court personally or he may appoint another to deal with the matter on his behalf, usually referred to as his attorney but not necessarily being a lawyer. At the hearing, the death of the tenant would be presented again stating whether or not he had made arrangements for its disposition. Usually a tenant surrendered his property, shortly after its acquisition, to the terms of his will. Quite often a will is recorded even though no record of probate can be found. This may then be the only record of such a deposition. It should be noted however that only the terms relevant to the inheritance of the heir are likely to be recorded in the text of the court record. A list of the deceased's property is then recited giving details of from whom it was purchased or inherited and when. A simple acquisition by purchase is not very helpful to the researcher but where the property has been inherited and reference is then made to the records at the date the inheritance was acquired by the deceased, then the chain starts all over again. Clearly then, a good set of records can take a line backwards to the ancestor who first purchased the property. One point to remember here however is that all manors had their own custom of descent of land. Whilst by far the majority of land passed to the eldest son, it was the custom of some manors, a custom known as Borough English, for the land to descend to the youngest son, a factor which once more widely known, will tend to turn upside-down the recognised history of our social mobility.

Records of changes in land ownership were not limited to heirs taking up their bequests. A simple sale of land from A to B will be recorded as a surrender from A and an admission to the land by B. Sometimes to raise money, or for reasons of convenience, copyholders mortgaged their property. Court records showed this as a CONDITIONAL SURRENDER and when the mortgage was repaid the mortgagor had to acknowledge satisfaction of the debt. Sometimes the mortgagee was unable to repay, and then the mortgagor applied to the lord to be admitted to the land as the new owner. . . These are all transactions with which we must be familiar today but recorded in the manorial records in a format unique until the Law of Property Act of 1922 and the Law of Property Amendment Act of 1924 which effectively abolished the copyhold form of tenure.

Using the latin records

You should by now begin to see that only certain parts of the text need concern you in a quest for family historical information. At either end of the later court books there should be an index of those tenants admitted to property. This should be checked and page references noted. If an ancestor sold property this will not be recorded in any index and it may prove necessary to search the whole book paragraph by paragraph if the entry has to be found. Most books and rolls do have marginal entries against the text where the new tenant has been admitted and this can prove useful in the absence of an index. The use of latin may prove a stumbling block at first but should not be regarded as an insurmountable barrier. Perhaps some of the greatest difficulties are caused by the use of abbreviations. No text-book can attempt to give a definitive guide to these and researchers must discover such local variations themselves. Not every record follows an identical pattern but the events before described do form the basis of what is covered and if the manual of court procedure has been followed there should be little difficulty in following the text.

The first heading is a simple one, merely identifying whether the proceedings are for the court leet (Curia Leta) or for the court baron (Curia Baron) both usually abbreviated to Cur. Leta and Cur. Baron. Remember that in later court books it is unlikely to find entries for the court leet as by this time the lord's judicial function had become almost meaningless. The lists of presentments that follow may be prefaced by PRESENTATUM EST QUOD, (It is presented that) COMPERTUM EST QUOD, (It is found that) both usually abbreviated to PRES.EST Q^{d} and COMP EST Q^{d}, or simply by the preface ITEM. At times the presentments will refer initially to the happenings of an earlier court and then the first words will be CUM AD CUR.(Whereas at a court. . .). (See Fig. 4). Shortly after this the first name should appear indicating who has done what. Where a tenant has died it is presented that at a previous court he surrendered (SURSUM-REDDIDIT – s'redd) the property. The phraseology used always refers here to the surrender being in the hands of the lord (IN MANUM DOMINI – MAN.DNI) by the hands of (PER MANUM-PER MAN.) the steward to the use of (AD OPUS) the last will and testament (ULTIME VOLUNTATIS – ULT. VOL) of the said (S^{d}) deceased date . . . . . of which the terms are as follows (VIZ:) The recital of the relevant extract of the will that follows is always in English so this is an easy part to identify. (Fig. 5) The applicant then begs the favour of the lord to be admitted to the property which is then itemised piece by piece. Sometimes the name of the land or property is given in English and this might help later identification, depending on the entry's proximity to the date of available tithe maps. Usually the names of landowners whose property borders on to that of the deceased are also given providing another clue in later identification. The deceased often acquired property from more than one source and the list of such holdings can often take up several pages of text. The important section to determine is at what point in the text does the listing from one source come to an end, for at this point the source, and the date of acqusition will be listed. These check-points are prefaced by the words

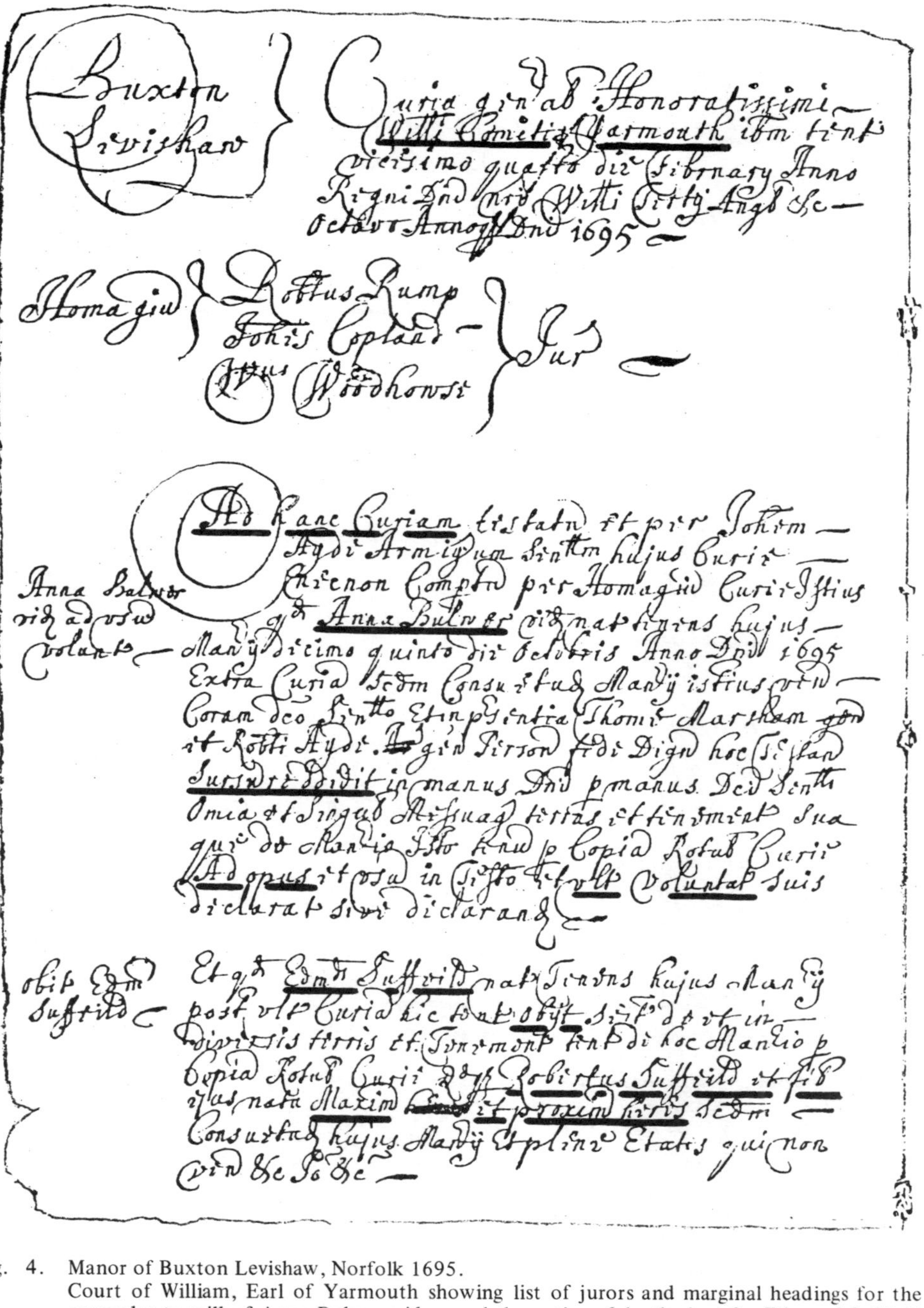

Buxton Levishaw

Curia gen(er)al(is) ab Honoratissimi Willi Comitis de Yarmouth ibm tent vicesimo quarto die Febrnary Anno Regni Dni nri Willi Tertij Angl &c Octavo Annoq Dni 1695

Homagiu — Robtus Rump, Johis Copland, Thus Woodhouse — Jur

Anna Bulwer rich ad usu volunt

Ad hanc Curiam testatu est per Johem Aydi Armigerum Sentm hujus Curie Et non compertu per Homagiu Curie istius qd Anna Bulwer vid nat tenens hujus Manerij decimo quinto die Octobris Anno Dni 1695 Extra Curiam secdm Consuetud Manerij istius vid Coram deo Sentto Et in psentia Thome Marsham gen et Robti Aydi [illegible] gen Person fide Dign hoc testan Sursum reddidit in manus Dni p manus dci Sentti Omia et singula Mesuag terras et tenemt sua que de Manio isto tenet p copia Rotul Curie Ad opus et usu in testo et ult voluntat suis declarat sive declarand

obit Edm Suffield

Et qd Edm Suffield nat tenens hujus Manerij post ult Curia hic tent obijt seit de et in diversis terris et tenemt tent de hoc Manio p copia Rotul Curie Et qd Robertus Suffield est fil ejus natu Maxim et proxim heres secdm Consuetud hujus Manerij Et plene Etatis qui non ven &c Io &c

Fig. 4. Manor of Buxton Levishaw, Norfolk 1695.
Court of William, Earl of Yarmouth showing list of jurors and marginal headings for the surrender to will of Anne Bulwer widow and the notice of death given for Edmund Suffield showing Robert Suffield as his eldest son and heir. (Reproduced by kind permission of C. W. Farrow Esq.)

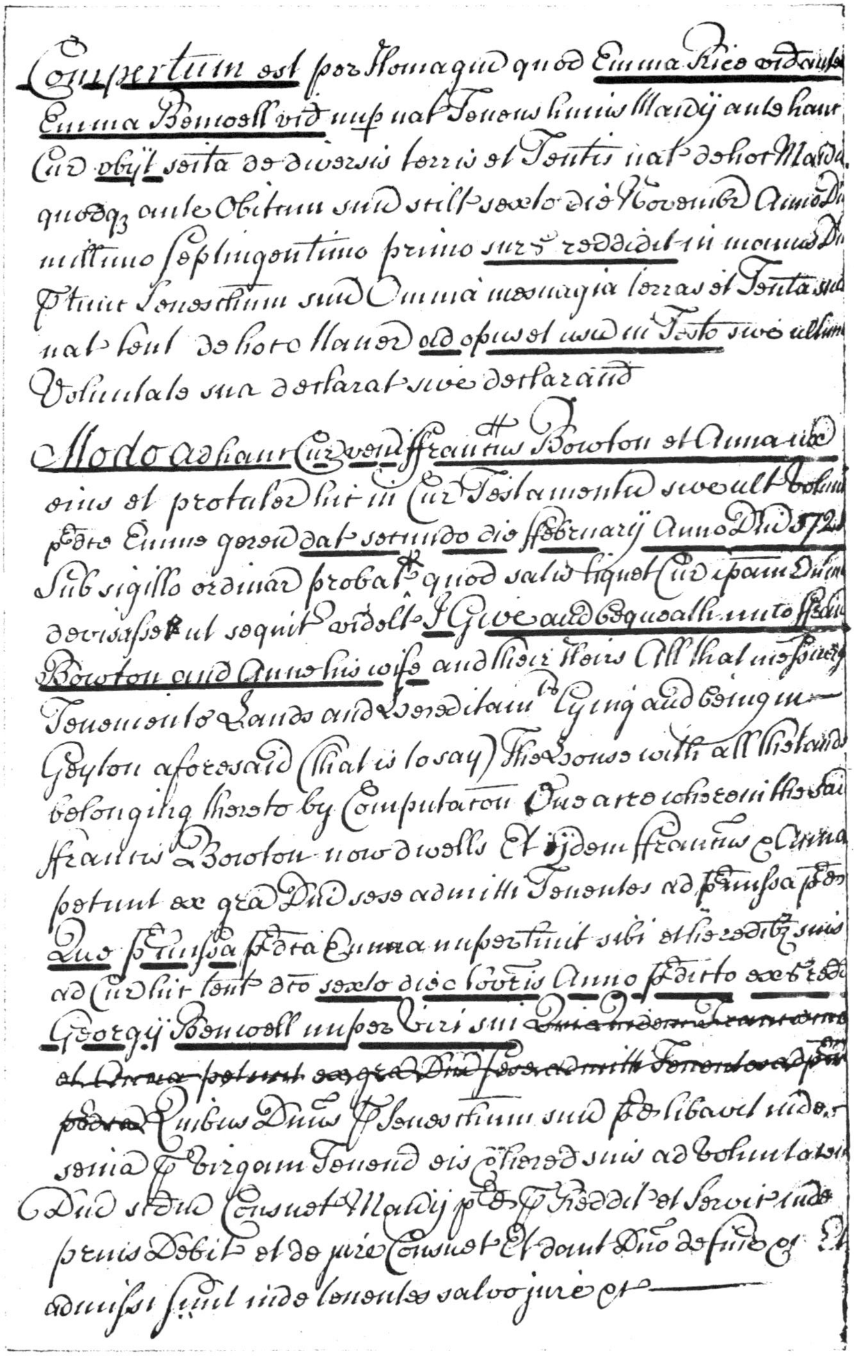

Compertum est per Homagium quod Emma Rice vidua nuper
Emma Benwell vid nup nat Tenens huius Manerij ante hanc
Cur obijt seita de diversis terris et Tentis nat dict Manerij
quodq ante Obitum suum scilt sexto die Novembr Anno Dni
millimo septingentesimo primo sursum reddidit in manus Dni
p Manus Tenentium suum Omnia mesuagia terras et Tenta sua
nat tent de dicto Manerio ad opus et usum in Testo suo ultim
Voluntate sua declarat sive declarand
Modo ad hanc Cur ven Franciscus Bowton et Anna ux
eius et protulerunt in Cur Testamentum sive ult volunt
pdce Emme gerend dat secundo die Februarij Anno Dni 1721
Sub sigillo ordinar probat quod satis liquet Cur ipam Dnam
devisasse ut sequitr videlt I Give and bequeath unto Francis
Bowton and Anne his wife and their Heirs All that messuage
Tenements Lands and hereditaments Lying and being in
Gayton aforesaid (that is to say) The House with all the lands
belonging thereto by Computation One acre whereon the said
Francis Bowton now dwells Et iidem Franciscus et Anna
petunt ex gra Dni sese admitti Tenentes ad pmissa pdca
Que pmissa pdca Emma nuper tenuit sibi et heredibus suis
ad Cur hic tent die sexto die Octobris Anno pdicto ex surs redd
Georgij Benwell nuper viri sui [struck through]
[struck through]
Quibus Dnus p Senescallum suum pdca liberavit inde
seisina p virgam Tenend eis et heredibus suis ad voluntatem
Dni secundum Consuet Manerij pdci p Reddit et Servit inde
prius Debit et de jure Consuet Et dant Dno de fine [illegible] Et
admissi sunt inde tenentes salvo jure et —

Fig. 5. Manor of Gayton, Norfolk 3rd Nov. 1723.
Presentment of death of Emma Rice w. formerly Emma Benwell w. having surrendered to will in 1701. Francis Bowton & his wife Ann brings Emma's will dated 1721, to court and are admitted to the property Emma had from her husband George Benwell.

QUE PREMISSA (Which premises) but the use of so many variant abbreviations for these words often makes it difficult to spot the entry. QUE may be written in full or may be simply written as 'Q'. PREMISSA is always abbreviated and may consist of any number of letters or flourishes following the 'p', for example Q' P'sa. (See Fig. 5) Then follows a description of how the deceased acquired the property usually taking it up to himself and his heirs (SIBI ET HERES), either on the death of (POST MORTEM) someone else or if he purchased the property, by the surrender (EX SURSEMREDD IT) of the named vendor. The date when all this happened should then be given but unfortunately this is not always done particularly in the earlier records, but where it is, then the family historian will derive his or her greatest satisfaction having been provided with the clue to search for the next generation.

With the case of a straightforward sale and purchase of land, the purchasers name is sometimes found in the earlier part of the text or after the full description of the lands being sold. The key words to look for here are AD OPUS (to the use of) which are usually written in capitals to highlight their importance and can quite easily be recognised, followed by the name of the purchaser. (See Fig. 4)

Those of you used to reading older wills may have come across the term NEPOS which may be interpreted as nephew or grandson. This is just as likely to be a problem in the will extracts found in the manorial records, even though the extract will be in English. When in Latin, this may be the only written interpretation of the deceased's intention and researchers must use other sources to determine the correct relationship.

A Working Example

To become more adept at interpreting the latin text it will prove useful to work through an actual example. Let us assume that you are researching the family of SIZER in Norfolk and that you have traced them to a village called Carlton south of Norwich: The Court records for that manor cannot be found so your only hope is to locate the court records of nearby manors whose holdings might have extended into Carlton.

The Docquet Books of the Manor of Kenninghall, situated not far from Carlton, give an indexed entry for the admission of Henry Sizer to property in 1694. The entry related to the admission is given in Fig. 6.

The first thing that appears as relevant is the marginal note, showing that soon after his admission, Henry sold the property in April 1695 to Peter Cole. Looking next at the latin text you will find that the details of the previous owner are given at the beginning of the text and not where you more often might expect to find them, nearer the end. Key phrases have been underlined but watch out for the many abbreviations.

To help you follow the text an English translation of all key phrases is given under the latin text.

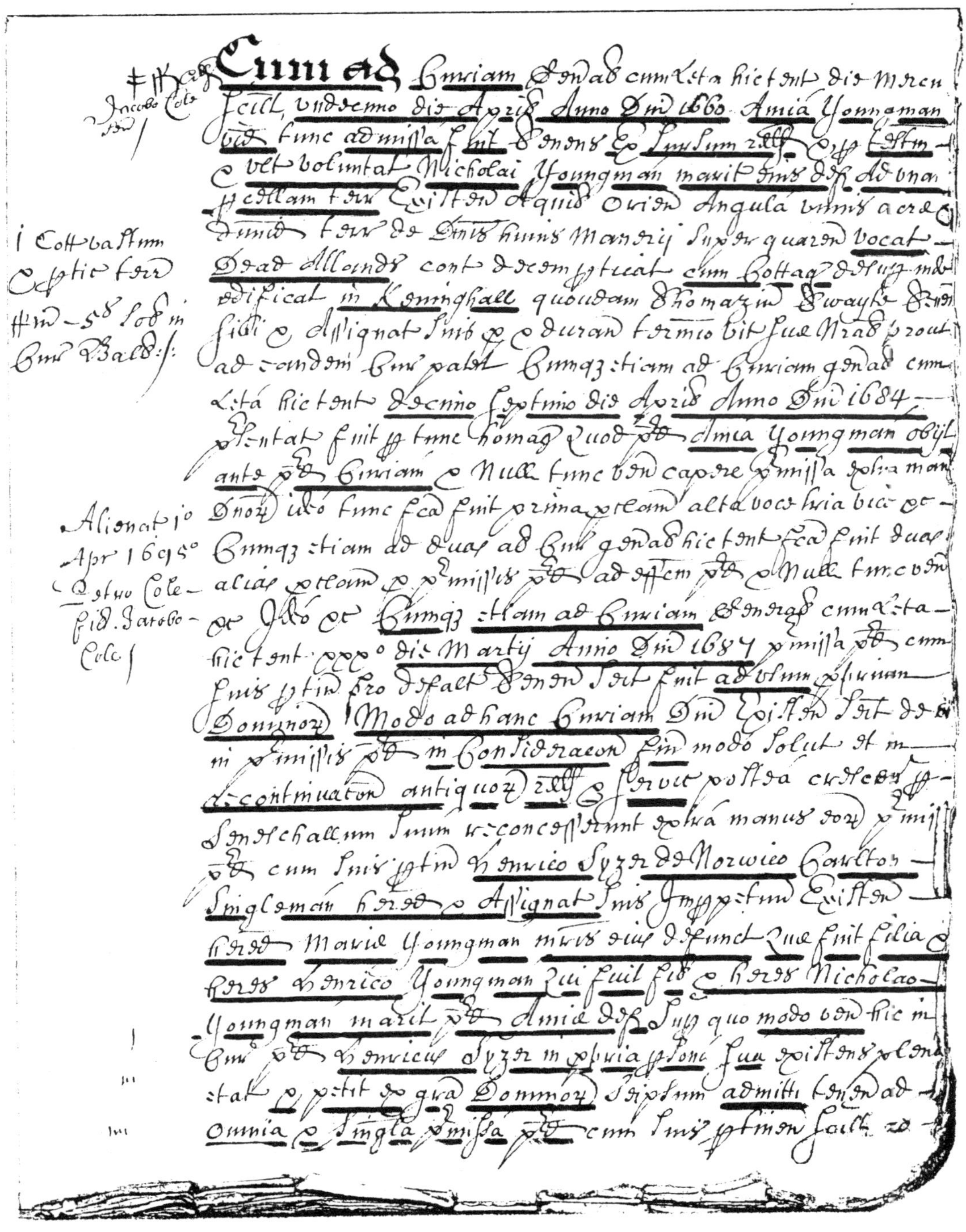

Fig. 6. Manor of Kenninghall, Norfolk 1694.
Admission of Henry Sizer.

Cum ad Curiam . . . tent(am) . . . undecimo die Apri^{s} Anno Dni Amia Youngman vid.
Whereas at a Court . . . held . . . 11th April (1660) Amy Youngman widow

admissa fuit tenens ex sursum reddit(ione) & p testim & ult(ime) voluntat(is)
was admitted a tenant by the surrender & by the last will & testament of

Nicholai Youngman marit(i) eius def(unct) . . ad . . . terr(a) . . vocat (Dead Allands . . . with a
Nicholas Youngman her husband deceased . . to . . . land . . . called

cottage . . . in Kenninghall) quondam Thomazin Thwayte tenens, sibi & assignat(is) suis
formerly Thomasine Thwaytes a tenant, her heirs & assigns

p & durante termino vite sue . . . Cumque etiam ad Curiam . . .
for & during the term of her life . . . Whereas also at a Court . . . (held 17th April 1684)

p'sentat(um) fuit p tunc homag(ium) quod p'd obiit ante p^{d}o Curiam
it was presented by the then homage that the said (Amy Youngman) died before the said Court

& null(us) tunc ven(it) capere p'missa . . prima p'clam . . . alta voce . . .
& no one then came to take the premisses . . first proclamation . . . in loud voice . . .

duas alias p'clam . . . null(us) tunc ven(it) . . . Cumque etiam ad Curiam
two other proclamations . . . no one came . . . Whereas also at a Court (30th March 1687)

p'missa p^{d} . . . pro defalt(a) tenen(tie) seit fuit ad usum . . . Dominor(um)
the said premises . . . by default of the tenancy was seized to the use of . . the Lords.

Modo ad hanc Curiam, Dni in considera(tione) fin(is) modo solu(ti), et in continua(tione) antiqor(um)
Now to this court, the Lord in consideration of a fine now paid, & in consideration of ancient

redd(itionum & servic(ii) postea crescen(tibus) p seneschallum suum reconcesserunt . . .
rights & services otherwise due through his steward regranted . . .

p'missa p^{d} cum suis p(er) tin(entibus)
the premises with their appurtenances (to Henry Syzer of Norwich Carlton singleman his heirs & assigns)

hered. Marie Youngman m(at)ris eius defunct que fuit filia & heres Henrico Youngman qui fuit fil & heres
heir of Mary Youngman his mother deceased who was daughter & heir of Henry Youngman who was

Nicholas Youngman marit. p^{d} Amia def. modo ven(it) Henricus Syzer
son & heir of Nicholas Youngman husband of the said Amy deceased. . . now comes Henry Syzer

in p'pria p'sona sua . . . & petit ex gra Dom. admitti tenens ad omnia & singla. p'missa p^{d} . . .
in his proper person & begs the favour of the Lord to be admitted to all & singular the said premisses . . .

This entry in itself provides us not only with a four generation pedigree but also gives other useful information. The entry initially refers to Amy's admission in 1660 so this entry must next be found in the appropriate book for that period.

The illustrated entry is given on pages 20 and 21. Falling just within the Commonwealth period, the entry fortunately appears in English.
Note the marginal entry on page 21 showing Henry Sizer's admission recorded for 1694.

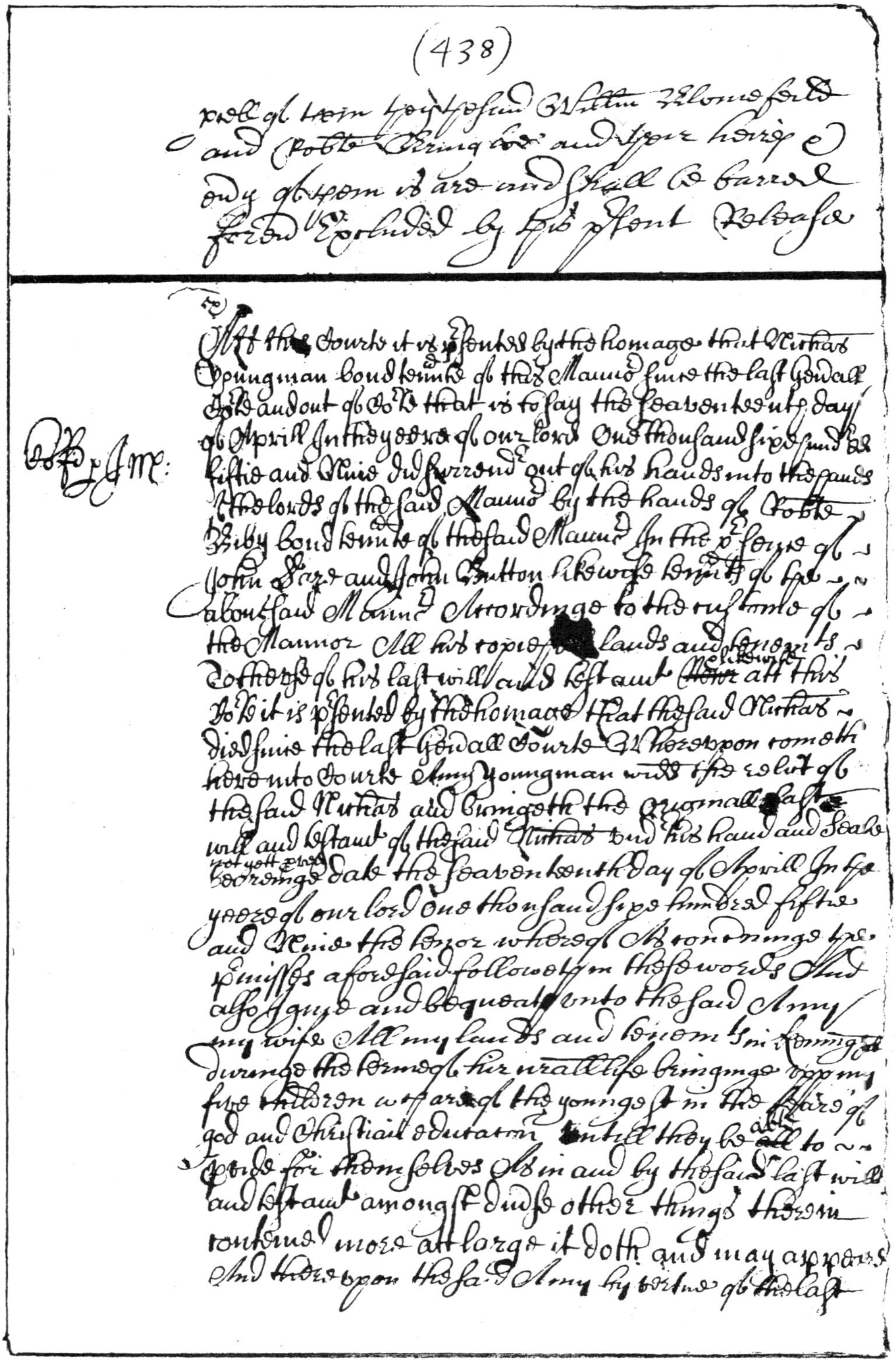

(438)

Reall of them the said Willm Blomefeild and Robte Kringe and their heires and every of them is are and shall be barred and Excluded by this present Release

[illegible]

Att this Courte it is presented by the homage that Richard Youngman bond tenante of this Mannor since the last Generall Courte and out of Courte that is to say the seaventeenth day of Aprill In the yeare of our lord One thousand sixe hundred fiftie and Nine did surrender out of his hands into the hands of the lords of the said Mannor by the hands of Robte Bixby bond tenante of the said Mannor In the presence of John Sayer and John Sutton likewise tenants of the above said Mannor According to the custome of the Mannor All his copie[hold] lands and tenements to the uses of his last will and testament Now att this Courte it is presented by the homage that the said Richard died since the last Generall Courte Whereupon cometh here into Courte Amy Youngman widdowe the relict of the said Richard and bringeth the originall last will and testament of the said Richard under his hand and seale not yett proved bearinge date the seaventeenth day of Aprill In the yeare of our lord One thousand sixe hundred fiftie and Nine the tenor whereof According to the premisses aforesaid followeth in these words And also I give and bequeath unto the said Amy my wife All my lands and tenements in Kenninghall during the terme of her naturall life bringinge upp my five children w[hi]ch are of the youngest in the feare of god and Christian education untill they be able to provide for themselves As in and by the said last will and testament amongst divers other things therein conteined more att large it doth and may appeare And thereupon the said Amy by vertue of the last

Fig. 7. Manor of Kenninghall 1660
Admission of Amy Youngman

11th April 1660

last will and testament aforesaid and of a surrender
to the use of the same craved to be admitted unto
One pightle of land lyinge the North east corner of
one acre and an halfe of lande of demeasnes of this
Manor upon a furlonge called Dead Mans
[illegible] lyinge [illegible] with a cottage thereupon
built in Kenninghall with said premisses the said
Richard Youngman late had [illegible] to him
and his heires of the surrender of Thomazine
[illegible] at a General Court here holden
the three and twentieth day of March In the
yeare of our lord one thousand five hundred
fiftie and eight Appeareth And she is
admitted thereof [illegible] to wit said Amy [illegible]
in full Court is delivered thereof seisin to hold to
her for and duringe the time of her naturall life
Accordinge to the forme and effect of the
last will and testament aforesaid by a rod
att the will of the lord Accordinge to the
custome of this Manor by the rents and
services therefor due and of right accustomed
and she giveth to the Lord for a fine [illegible]
her fathers [illegible] Savinge [illegible]
Man his right

(margin) 1 Cott 2 pightles
(margin) [illegible] adm. 1694
(margin) The admission of Amy Youngman

Att this Court cometh Thomas [illegible] a Copyhold
tenant of this Manor and in full Court [illegible] surrender
out of his hands into the hands of the lord of
the said Manor by the hands of the Steward
two acres and an halfe of land att [illegible] in
one pightell And halfe an acre in the same
furlonge [illegible] with the lands of Charles
Watts And one acre lyinge att Upper grave

(margin) [illegible]
(margin) 2 acr. [illegible] [illegible]

Fig. 8. Manor of Kenninghall 1660
Admission of Amy Youngman, page 2.

From the two court entries, the following brief pedigree can be constructed:

NICHOLAS YOUNGMAN Purchased prop. of Manor of Kenninghall ex Thomasine Thwayte 1658. Dead 1660 (ct. bk) Will date 17.4.1659 = AMY living 1659, Admitted her husbands prop. 1660. dead 1684

HENRY YOUNMAN mentioned as son and heir 1694 (ct. bk) married . . . . . .

child living 1659

child living 1659

child living 1659

child living 1659

Mary Youngman, dau. & h. dead 1694. m. .... SIZER

HENRY SIZER of Norwich Carlton, Adm. Kenninghall prop. as son & heir of mother 1964 which he sold 1695 to Peter Cole.

When a new tenant applied to the court to be admitted the steward had to satisfy himself that the applicant had good title. The steward would then refer to the entry in the court record to show his entitlement and would often make a marginal note against that entry giving the name of the new owner with date of his admission.

The text follows the same pattern, with the presentment of Nicholas Youngman surrendering to his will at the last court (1659). Amy, the widow, then brings to court her husbands will dated 17th April 1659 which gives a life interest in the property to Amy asking her to bring up his five children until they can look after themselves. In itself this is an important discovery. Nicholas's will was actually proved in 1661 but it has never been found. The entry here then probably represents the only known version of what was written.

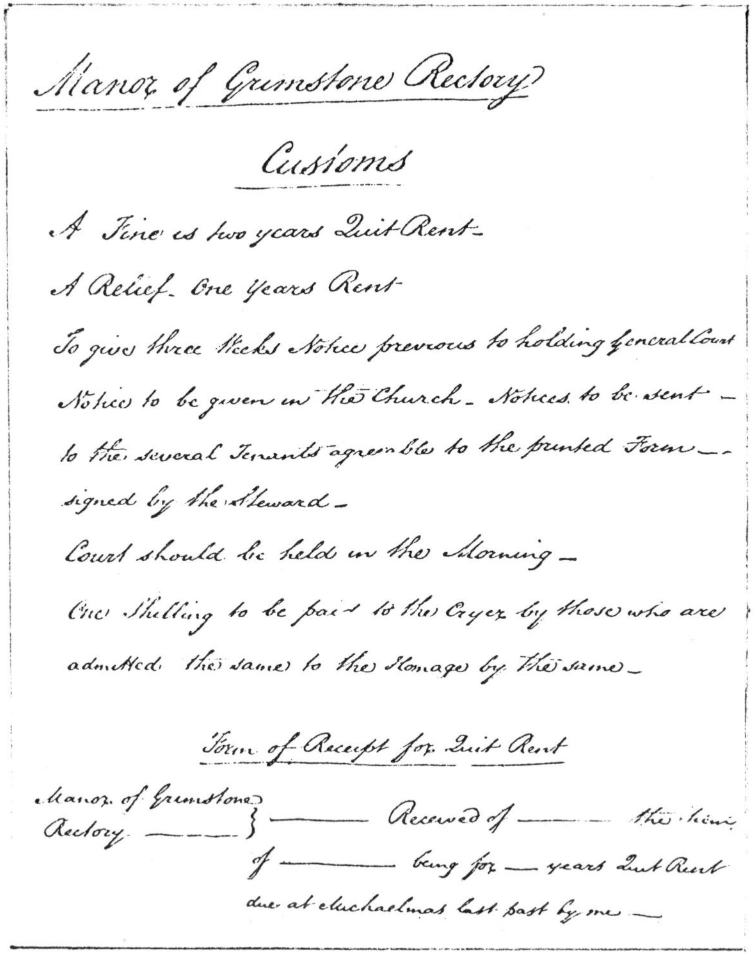

Manor of Grimstone Rectory

Customs

A Fine is two years Quit Rent –

A Relief – One Years Rent

To give three Weeks Notice previous to holding General Court

Notices to be given in the Church – Notices to be sent –

to the several Tenants agreeable to the printed Form –

signed by the Steward –

Court should be held in the Morning –

One Shilling to be paid to the Cryer by those who are

admitted the same to the Homage by the same –

Form of Receipt for Quit Rent

Manor of Grimstone Rectory } ——— Received of ——— the sum

of ——— being for — years Quit Rent

due at Michaelmas last past by me —

Fig. 9. Manor of Grimston Rectory mid. 18th. c.
Customs of the Manor.

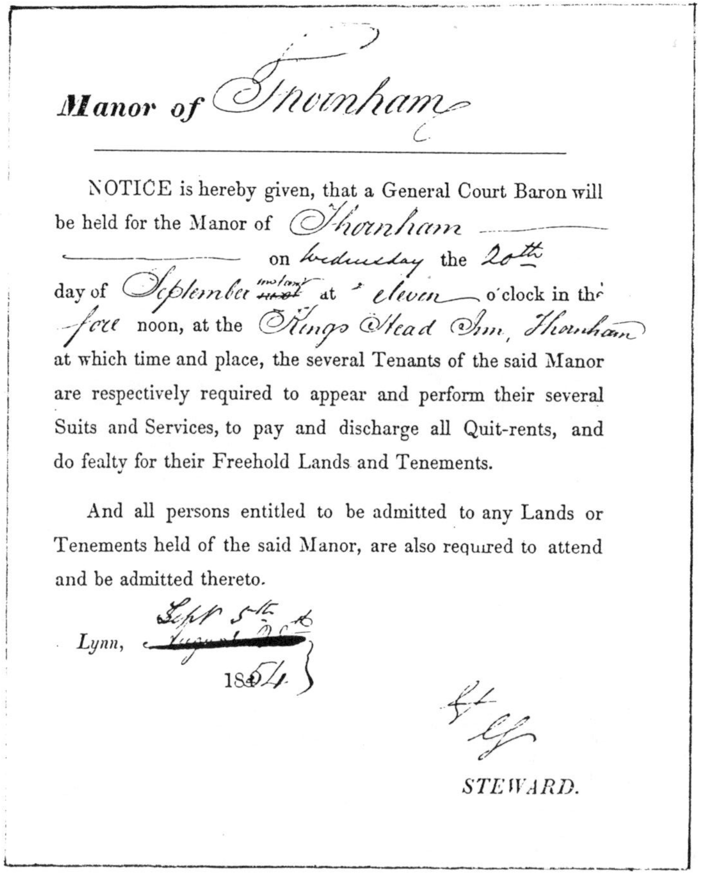

Manor of Thornham

NOTICE is hereby given, that a General Court Baron will be held for the Manor of Thornham ——— on Wednesday the 20th day of September instant ~~next~~ at eleven o'clock in the fore noon, at the Kings Head Inn, Thornham at which time and place, the several Tenants of the said Manor are respectively required to appear and perform their several Suits and Services, to pay and discharge all Quit-rents, and do fealty for their Freehold Lands and Tenements.

And all persons entitled to be admitted to any Lands or Tenements held of the said Manor, are also required to attend and be admitted thereto.

Lynn, Sept 5th [redacted] 1854

STEWARD.

Fig. 10. Manor of Thornham 1854 Notice of a Court to be held
(Ex Libris Norfolk & Norwich Genealocical Society)

It is always wise to check the earlier entry showing when and how the first known ancestor acquired the property. In this case, the entry for 1658 merely states that Nicholas purchased the property for £10 but it might as easily have described Nicholas, in that part of the text showing to whose use the property was surrendered, as Nicholas Youngman of Carlton Yeoman.

In general, the older the document, the more difficult at first glance does the text seem to decipher. In reality, there are few variations in presentation and format throughout the centuries and a little patience and perseverance and especially practice, will soon enable the beginner to become adept enough to determine at least the salient points of any court extract.

It is somewhat incredulous to believe that all heirs to property managed to come forward and claim their inheritance. Obviously, in many cases this did not happen and the property reverted to the Lord. In the example just given (page 18) we learned that Amy Youngman had died by 1684 but that no heirs came forward. Again three years later, still no one came. Presumably, it was not until 1694 that Henry Sizer learned of his inheritance, a gap of some ten years. In an age of widespread illiteracy, perhaps this is not so surprising and as those so entitled lived far away from their property, it could not always have been general knowledge just who were the heirs still less where they lived. Undoubtedly, in the early centuries

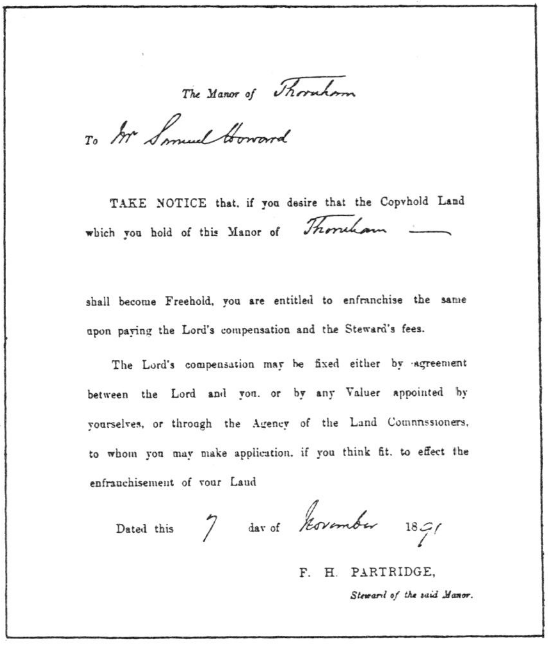

The Manor of Thornham

To Mr Samuel Howard

TAKE NOTICE that, if you desire that the Copyhold Land which you hold of this Manor of Thornham ——

shall become Freehold, you are entitled to enfranchise the same upon paying the Lord's compensation and the Steward's fees.

The Lord's compensation may be fixed either by agreement between the Lord and you, or by any Valuer appointed by yourselves, or through the Agency of the Land Commissioners, to whom you may make application, if you think fit, to effect the enfranchisement of your Land

Dated this 7 day of November 1891

F. H. PARTRIDGE,
Steward of the said Manor.

Fig. 11. Manor of Thornham 1891
Invitation to tenant to enfranchise copyhold. (Ex Libris Norfolk & Norwich Genealogical Society)

when most of the tenants lived in a closely defined area, notice was passed by word of mouth and perhaps by notice in the parish church. In more recent centuries, the advent of newspaper circulation and the use of the printed word generally, played a more significant part in advertising future court hearings. At times, you will find at the commencement of a court book, a list of special customs of the manor. Now each manor had its own customs most of which were fairly standard. Occasionally however, you will find such differing customs as descent by gavelkind, notably in Kent, where property of a deceased is shared, or descent by Borough English, notably in East Anglia where property descended to the youngest son, not the eldest. The customs of the Manor of Grimston Rectory in Norfolk (fig. 9) show that 3 weeks notice had to be given to tenants both in the parish church and on a prescribed printed form. Fig. 10 shows an example of such a standard printed form used for the Manor of Thornham in Norfolk as late as 1854.

Even by the middle of the eighteenth century the manorial system had greatly changed from the time when a Lord's holdings were spread amongst a large number of his tenants. More and more of the larger landowners increased their holdings at the expense of the small farmer, who often sank into degradation. By the nineteenth century, the manorial land was held by a mere handful of tenants, much of the original land having been gradually enfranchised. Tenants were actually invited to enfranchise their land on payment to the Lord of the necessary fees (Fig. 11).

No study of the subject of this brevity can expect to give definitive answers to all the problems raised by styles and procedures which varied as much by their localisation as by the hands which compiled the records within each locality. Basically however, rules of court procedure were clearly laid down and manuals used by court stewards should have ensured a high degree of uniformity in procedure. Like most fields of study, patience and determination are likely to be rewarded and it will surprise many sceptics eventually, just how adept they can become through perseverance.